Prairie Sunrise

My Montana Ranch Life

Prairie Sunrise

My Montana Ranch Life

by Sierra Dawn

for all the Prairie Roses of Timber Creek

Published by the author.

Hi, my name is Zora Rose, which means Dawn Flower.

I am six, and I live on a ranch on the prairie in Montana.

I live here with my grandma and grandpa, my mommy and daddy, and my little brother, Linden. He's four.

My great great grandparents and my great great great grandma Belle started the ranch almost a hundred years ago.

The first ranch house was a cabin that Great Great Grandad McKee built. (That is Mommy and my aunt when they were little girls.)

Ranchers have a very, very important job called moving the big grazers. Prairies have a lot of grass. Grazers eat grass, and grass eats sunshine, because it's a plant. Every year the old grass stems and leaves die. If a grazer never eats them, they shade the new leaves, and the grass starves to death. But grazers like to eat the same grass over and over if no one moves them. That kills the grass, too

This is in September. Winter is coming, and most of the grass leaves are dead. This grass is on a steep hill by the house. The only grazers we let around the house are horses, and they do not climb the steep hills as much as cows do, so this grass has years and years of dead leaves. My calico friend Emmeline does not eat grass, but she is interested in the things that interest me.

Everywhere there are grasslands, someone
has to move the big grazers. Sometimes, it is
big animals, like lions. I asked Mommy if there
were dinosaurs that had to move the big
dinosaur grazers. She said she didn't know.
There wasn't any grass then, but maybe.

In the old, old days, where our ranch is, people called the Pikuni had our job. Their grazers were bison, and they used fire and runners to move them. Our grazers are cows, and we move them with horses and fences.

We learn about the Before People in school. It's hard work to live on the prairie, and people have to be smart to move big grazers. So it's important to respect them and learn from them. That's what Mommy says.

When you move a herd with horses, there are different jobs. The jobs have names from the old days when cowboys moved big herds of cows a long way. The person beside the front of the herd is riding point. Swing is behind point, flank is behind swing, and drag is behind the herd.

Grandma Rose is riding swing on little Jenny. Jenny is sweet, but she is young, so she is silly sometimes.

The old time cowboys had just one job, like Lindy and me. We ride drag. I didn't know if I liked having the follow behind job, but Mommy said that is the job for little kids. That is the job she had when she was six. So then I was happy, because I want to be just like Mommy.

We take a small herd a short way, so there is no flank rider. Grandma, Grandpa, and Mommy go between point and swing and sometimes drag.

Linden is on Riesgo and I am on Trisca.

I always want to be good help and be in the right place, but it's hard. Mommy says that it takes a long time to know where to be. My horse Trisca is really smart. I call her my pretty pony. She knows all about cows.

Trisca used to be Grandma Rose's horse, but I think she likes to be my horse. She nickers when she sees me. Even if I don't know where to be, Trisca does. Then people say, "You were good help." I like that best of all.

There are lots of rules to remember about herding cows. Everyone has had to learn them since Great Great Grandad McKee first had cows here.

Don't turn your back to the herd. Don't ride between someone else and the herd. Don't make a cow that is being a good girl trot. Don't go so fast that you pass a calf; he will get scared and run away. I try to remember all the rules, but sometimes I forget some.

Linden's Riesgo has a big white stripe on his face. It's called a blaze. Trisca just has a little star. Riesgo is Trisca's big brother. Their great grandmother, Coffee, was my great grandad Bill's horse. Their grandmother, Foxy Filly was Mommy's horse when she was our age. Mommy and Foxy rode drag on this same trail behind these same calves' great great great great grandmas. Sometimes I pretend I am Mommy and Trisca is Foxy.

Our friend Nový Den helps us chase the cows. Her name means "new day" in Czech. When Great Grandad Bill died, Grandpa and Grandma got a new puppy and moved to the ranch to live. It was a new day for them.

Nový is like me. She likes herding cows better than anything, and she wants to be good help. Nový knows a lot about cows. But sometimes she forgets the rules. She forgets that cows being good should not trot. Or she gets confused and chases the cows the wrong way. That causes problems. Then Grandma Rose yells.

Sometimes we just move the cows, and sometimes we give them medicine. The calves have to have shots to protect them from nasty diseases, just like little kids. They get really scared, because they are not used to people. They live on the open prairie all year long like the deer. They never see a person up close before they get their shots.

When Linden and I get our shots, we are brave and don't cry. Not all the calves are that brave. They are scared and do not understand about shots.

Linden hates to see anyone cry. He tells the calves, "Don't be scared. You'll be back with your mommy soon."

I like to understand things, so I tell them, "You need your shots so you won't get nasty diseases. You don't want a nasty disease."

The best part is if our friend, Lady, has the "stay out of the way" job, too. Horse Day Spa is her favorite game. If we stand on the vaccine table, we are tall enough to brush and braid her mane for her.

We wear helmets when we ride our horses. They protect our heads if we fall off. Linden has fallen off more than I have.

We wear straw hats on top of our helmets. They protect our heads, too. The sun is very bright and hot on the prairie. There are no trees for shade. All that bright sun can make your head hurt if you forget your hat.

This year, I had a really important job when the cows got their shots. I pulled a chain to open a little gate so the cows could go into the alley. Then I let go and closed the gate behind them.

I have to open and shut the gate just right. If I am slow, the cows are already coming when I open the gate. They see it move and get scared. Then they don't want to go stand in the alley. If I am too slow to close it, one of the cows might back out. Then she would be by herself. When the cows are by themselves, they get scared, and they can hurt themselves or someone else.

The cows got their shots while they stood in line in the alley. Then Grandpa Ron let them out, and I let the next bunch in.

It is very important to work quickly and quietly so the cows stay happy.

The catwalk is a high, narrow board that Grandma Rose walks on when she gives the cows shots. Grandma Rose studied to be a veterinarian in college. That means she is an animal doctor. Lindy and I have to stay down so we don't scare the cows coming into the alley.

But if you climb onto the back of the catwalk just when Grandpa Ron opens the headgate and then walk toward the headgate, it helps the cows know to walk quietly out. That is a job Linden can do, but sometimes he forgets. He is still little.

Then Mommy and Daddy go back for shovels and tubs. We dig up all the foxtail and take it away to burn or dump where it can't grow.

Linden and I are really good at spotting Garrison creeping foxtail. It is an important job, because the big people might not see every plant. Every plant we don't dig up makes a lot of seeds. That is a lot of work for next year.

It's hard work. We have to walk a long way. But it is fun to spend all day with Daddy. We get to have a picnic and play in the dirt. We see neat things like damsel flies.

This is when I was two. I'm playing in the Maximilian sunflowers. They are really beautiful. They are not selfish at all. Mommy counts lots and lots of other plants growing with them. They smell like chocolate. I can even smell them from Trisca. Garrison creeping foxtail would not let them grow here. We work to protect them, because we don't want them to be gone. We like them a lot.

We also find leopard frogs. Five kinds of frogs and toads live on the ranch. Frogs are really important. A lot of places have gotten so polluted that frogs can't live there anymore. So we have to take extra good care of our frogs.

These elk are near where we dig up the foxtail. Garrison creeping foxtail isn't good elk food, but the plants that grow in the creek now are. Our work protects the elk, too. They are pretty to see.

Things like elk and rabbits and deer are little grazers. Little grazers like grass that has been grazed recently. If the big grazers move, the little grazers move, too.

In July, we have another really important job. We monitor. That means we ask the Land if we have been moving the grazers right. Listening to the Land is hard work. We take a lunch and work all day for a week. It is really fun, but sometimes we get hot and tired. We have to walk a long way to our sites.

Mommy and Daddy monitor. Mommy studied botany in college. That means she knows about plants. Daddy studied math. So Mommy writes down the names of the plants, and Daddy counts them. But Daddy knows the plants, too. And Mommy can count.

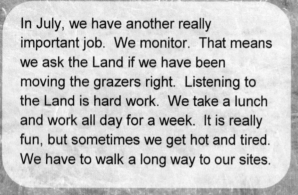

At the site we have to see everything and write it on a data sheet. Data is what you notice and write down. When I was four, I found something really important at a site. I found a nest. The baby birds had hatched and gone away. We wrapped a piece of shell in a Kleenex and took it home to Grandpa Ron. He studied zoology in college, so he knows about animals. He said it was a duck egg shell. Mommy wrote down my data.

I noticed something important this year, too. I saw a rattlesnake that the big people hadn't seen. So I yelled, "Rattlesnake!" and pointed. It had just shed its skin. The skin was lying right there.

Sometimes we find rare plants or things like baby cactus just out of their seeds. Mommy gets really excited about rare plants. I think they are neat, too.

Shedding makes rattlesnakes grumpy. They are dangerous when they are grumpy, just like cows. The rattlesnake crawled into a gopher hole. Linden and I like to play with snake skins, but we didn't play with that one. You have to be careful where there are rattlesnakes.

This year, I could write my numbers, so I got to write on a real data sheet, not just a pretend one like Linden. Daddy counted grass stems, and I wrote down the number. The data sheet had a table of little boxes. Every number had to be written in the right box. But I can read, so I knew where to write the numbers.

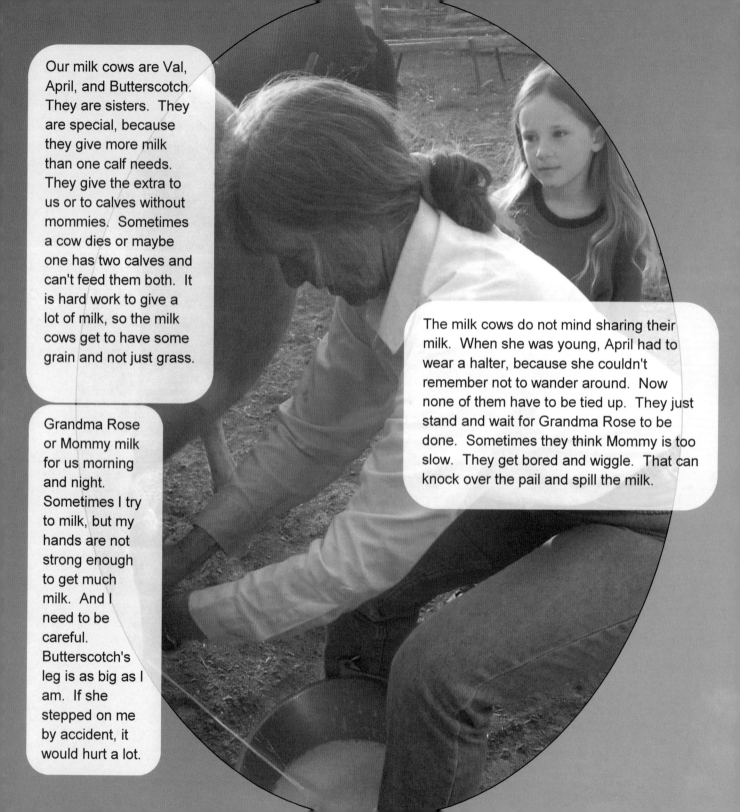

Our milk cows are Val, April, and Butterscotch. They are sisters. They are special, because they give more milk than one calf needs. They give the extra to us or to calves without mommies. Sometimes a cow dies or maybe one has two calves and can't feed them both. It is hard work to give a lot of milk, so the milk cows get to have some grain and not just grass.

Grandma Rose or Mommy milk for us morning and night. Sometimes I try to milk, but my hands are not strong enough to get much milk. And I need to be careful. Butterscotch's leg is as big as I am. If she stepped on me by accident, it would hurt a lot.

The milk cows do not mind sharing their milk. When she was young, April had to wear a halter, because she couldn't remember not to wander around. Now none of them have to be tied up. They just stand and wait for Grandma Rose to be done. Sometimes they think Mommy is too slow. They get bored and wiggle. That can knock over the pail and spill the milk.

When there are a lot of flies, they bite the milk cows. The cows can't stand still when they are being bitten, so someone has to swat flies for them. That is a job I can do. When I was five, my friend Little Brown Face liked it if I swatted his flies, too.

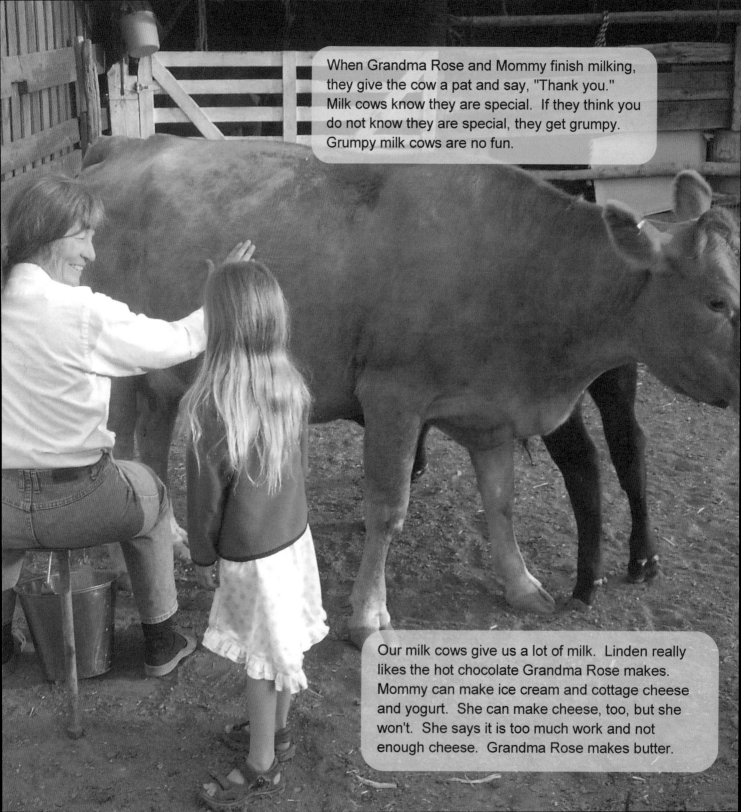

When Grandma Rose and Mommy finish milking, they give the cow a pat and say, "Thank you." Milk cows know they are special. If they think you do not know they are special, they get grumpy. Grumpy milk cows are no fun.

Our milk cows give us a lot of milk. Linden really likes the hot chocolate Grandma Rose makes. Mommy can make ice cream and cottage cheese and yogurt. She can make cheese, too, but she won't. She says it is too much work and not enough cheese. Grandma Rose makes butter.

We strain the milk through a cloth in case any dust or hair fell into it. Then we cool it in water before we put it into the refrigerator.

Linden and I help make ice cream and butter. To make butter, you put cream in a churn. The churn has a big wooden paddle. You turn the handle, and the paddle mixes and mixes the cream until it turns into butter.

The milk is warm and frothy when it comes out of the cow.

To make ice cream, you have to save snow from winter. This was when I was five. We didn't have much snow last winter, so we couldn't make ice cream this year.

Butter is from cream. Some cows' cream is easier to turn into butter and some cows' cream is easier to turn into whipped cream. Val is a butter cow, and April is a whipped cream cow. When Mommy was a little girl, Ashley's cream wouldn't turn into butter at all, so they never had cow butter.

Butterscotch is the littlest milk cow. She is the baby sister. She does not look like the other cows. She is a different color and her face is crooked.

Grandma Rose was afraid Butterscotch had hurt her face, but Mommy checked her baby pictures, and she was born that way. Sometimes that happens. Butterscotch was born when I was three.

The other cows did not like Butterscotch because she looked different. She didn't have any friends, and she was sad.

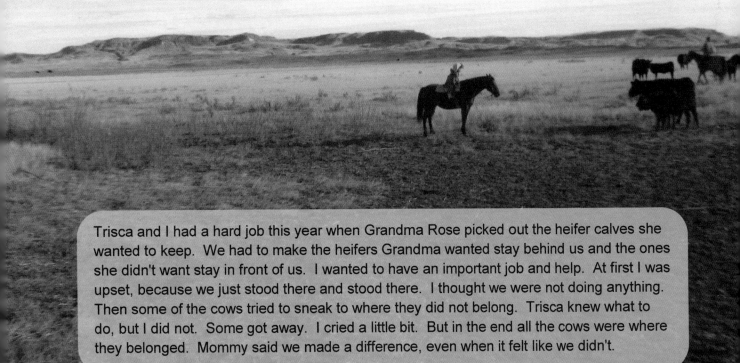

Every year, the little girl calves have to learn to be big girl calves. Girl calves are called heifers. When they are calves, they go everywhere their mommies do and do everything their mommies tell them. They have to learn to be their own cows and make their own choices. When it's time for the heifers to grow up, Grandma and Grandpa leave the mother cows on the range and bring the heifer calves to a pasture near the house.

Trisca and I had a hard job this year when Grandma Rose picked out the heifer calves she wanted to keep. We had to make the heifers Grandma wanted stay behind us and the ones she didn't want stay in front of us. I wanted to have an important job and help. At first I was upset, because we just stood there and stood there. I thought we were not doing anything. Then some of the cows tried to sneak to where they did not belong. Trisca knew what to do, but I did not. Some got away. I cried a little bit. But in the end all the cows were where they belonged. Mommy said we made a difference, even when it felt like we didn't.

Grandma Rose puts Butterscotch with the new heifers. The new heifers are little and scared. Everything is strange for them. They miss their mommies. Butterscotch knows lots of things. She teaches the heifers how to be their own cows.

Once the heifers know they have grown up, they go back with their mothers. Their mothers and aunts teach them about the range and plants and weather. Their mothers tell them, "Stay away from that cow. She is strange and does not look like us." And the heifers say, "No. That is Butterscotch. She is our teacher. She is smart. She looks different, but she is beautiful and special. She is our friend." Now Butterscotch has lots of friends, and she is happy.

Miss Piggy was Val's calf this year. She is really friendly. She comes up behind you and licks you to make you pet her. I liked playing with her when she was little. She makes me a little nervous now. She is so big. I'm not sure she knows how heavy her feet are.

I think Patches is beautiful, but I do not really like calf kisses. Patches' mommy had two calves and Patches got lost. Grandma and Grandpa found her and gave her to Olive Oil. Olive Oil has enough milk to be a milk cow, but she doesn't want to. But she liked Patches. Patches liked having enough to eat and a new brother. She always remembers that people helped her when she was alone and scared and hungry, so she likes people.

Patches and Miss Piggy have an important job. They are with the new heifers. The little heifers are wild, and they think people are scary. Patches says, "Oh, those are just people. They are not scary. I know all about people." Then the other calves stop being afraid.

The cows have to take care of themselves on the prairie. They have to be smart and careful. But it is bad for them to be scared. When they are scared, they aren't happy, and they can get hurt. So Patches teaches them not to be afraid of people.

In the winter, we have to put our clothes on racks in the basement to dry. But in the summer, we hang them outside on the clothesline.

I have helped hang up clothes since I was a baby (this is when I was two), but now I can reach the clothesline. I helped to hang out the clothes for my very first recess ever, but usually I play at recess.

I used to have a little kitty all my own. Her name was Salem.

We didn't know it when we got her, but Salem was very sick. Grandma Rose tried hard to save her. She kept Emmeline from getting sick, but she couldn't save Salem. Salem got sicker and sicker and then she died.

Mommy says, "The animals think we are magic. They think we can do anything. But we are just people. We can only try our best."

I wish Grandma was magic. I miss Salem a lot. Emmeline is healthy and beautiful and sweet. She likes to play. Even when Salem was well enough to play with me, she only wanted to play quiet games like Pirate Ship and Kitty Scarf. But everyone is Emmeline's favorite person. Salem's favorite person was just me.

Salem is buried by the clothes line. Sometimes when Mommy hangs out the clothes, I go to see Salem. I tell her what I am doing now. I tell her I miss her. I tell her I am glad she was my kitty. Sometimes I cry. It's OK to cry when sad things happen.

When I was five, there was a Hard Winter. Snow and ice covered all the grass. The cows could not find enough to eat on the prairie. (This is Grandma Rose. Little people don't have to ride in Hard Winters, but big people do. Grandma Rose rode my good, brave Trisca. Grandpa and Grandma fought the snow to save the cows.)

There have always been Hard Winters. Mommy read all the old stories. She counted all the Hard Winters for 150 years. There were ten.

In the old, old days, Hard Winters were very bad. When the Pikuni had Hard Winters, they had to watch a lot of their animals die. The people died, too. It was hard and sad. When my great grandparents and great great grandparents had Hard Winters, half their animals died. The people would be hungry and cold.

Hard Winters are still hard. A lot of the wild animals die. We can help them a little, but not much. When we move our grazers right, the prairie is healthy. Having a healthy prairie helps them most of all.

Some of the cows die. High Horns fell on the ice and died. We were sad. Girlie was born in the Hard Winter. Her feet hurt whenever it is cold. Great Grandad Bill built a barn into the hillside so the horses that worked in winter would have a warm place to be. Girlie asks to spend the night there when it is cold. The other range cows never go into a barn. Girlie's feet will never get all better. (The gray horse is Curio. Maxine's son really liked her, so Grandma Rose traded her to him for little Jenny.)

Even people die sometimes. Great Grandad Bill
died the Hard Winter before I was born.

But we are grateful to live in the new days when Hard Winters are easier. Grandpa and Grandma went out to the range and brought the cows home. They had to walk on the ridges, where there was less snow. The cows were confused. They had never left the range before. It was hard, cold work. Trisca was very brave.

People that live by rivers can grow a lot of hay.
Grandma and Grandpa bought stacks of hay. A
big truck brought it. Most of the winter, the snow
was so deep that no one could drive on the road.
But sometimes a big plow would come. Then a
truck would bring hay, and we could get
groceries. In the old days, people couldn't leave
in a Hard Winter. They couldn't get help from
outside until spring.

Grandpa Ron took the tractor and carried the
hay to the cows. The cows didn't know what
hay was, but they learned fast. They had to.

Mommy says that I will be big when the next Hard Winter comes. I will fight the snow and try to save the cows. Some of them will die. Then I will say, "I tried my best." I will look like Grandma Rose when I say it. I will be as cold and tired as a person can be. And I will be sad.

But spring will come. When spring comes, there will be green grass, and sunshine, and new baby calves. Because even Hard Winters end.

In a Hard Winter, we need trucks and trucks full of hay for all the cows. We can't grow that much hay. But we can grow a little hay. We can grow enough for the milk cows and the horses that work in winter.

Linden likes to pretend that he is Grandpa Ron swathing hay.

Grandpa Ron cuts the hay with Great Grandad Bill's old swather.

Grandpa Ron rakes the hay next. The rake makes bunches of hay.

Sometimes it rains on the hay. Then we have to stack it in little cones so it will dry out. Grandpa Ron knows all about hay. He tells everyone else what they need to do. (This is when I was four and my cousin helped us.)

Then, we all pile the bunches or cones of hay onto a pickup with pitch forks. Grandpa Ron drives it to Great Grandad Bill's barn.

We make tall stacks of hay on top of the barn. Grandpa Ron tells everyone how to stack the hay.

We all help.

The hay has to be stacked very tightly so that rain can't run down into the stack. If rain runs into the stack, the hay molds. Everyone's work is ruined.

Linden and I jump on the stack to pack it tightly. (This is when I was four.) Then Grandpa Ron makes a top that the rain will run off of. Now the hay is ready for winter.

We can play on the hay the next summer if it isn't too likely to rain. Playing on the hay can punch holes in Grandpa Ron's top. Then the water can run in and ruin the hay. But we can play on the stack that Grandma Rose is feeding to the horses if she thinks it won't rain before they eat it all. Sometimes she guesses wrong.

We need electricity at the ranch so we can have lights and a computer. Mommy showed us how the wind blows power across the prairie and spins the wind mill. (Real wind mills pump water or grind wheat. This is really a wind generator because it makes electricity. But wind mill is easier to say.) The wind mill sends power down the hill and into the house so we can plug in the refrigerator. Linden said, "The wind plugs in!"

We have solar panels, too, so we can get electricity from the sun.

When the moon is full, you can see shadows and some colors. You can see red and sometimes blue. You can read. But you can't take a picture of anything but the moon by moonlight. Mommy tries all the time, and it never works.

On the prairie, the moon and stars are very beautiful. Sometimes we have falling stars or northern lights. They are green. Mommy can't take pictures of stars and northern lights, but she can take pictures of the moon and planets. The planets in this picture are Venus and Jupiter, I think. They are kind of hard to see.

Sometimes Daddy gets out his telescope and we look at the moon and stars. My favorite are the Pleiades. Sirius is pretty, because he blinks red and blue and green. Saturn has rings. Jupiter has tiny little moons like sparkles of pixie dust. Daddy says we have to watch the moon and stars and remember them for the rest of our lives, because most of the places people live don't have a sky where you can see stars. I can't imagine a place like that.

The ranch has lots of birds. Birds like the prairie.
My favorite are the swallows. Swallows eat
mosquitoes, so they are very important to us.

The swallows build nests on the house.
Snakes eat their babies, and snakes can't climb
the house walls. But it is hard to make mud
stick to the wall. The nests fall down. So
Grandpa Ron tied one nest onto the wall with a
strip of sturdy plastic and nailed a piece of
board under it to hold it up. The swallows like
that nest now. They can fill it full of heavy
babies, and it won't fall down.

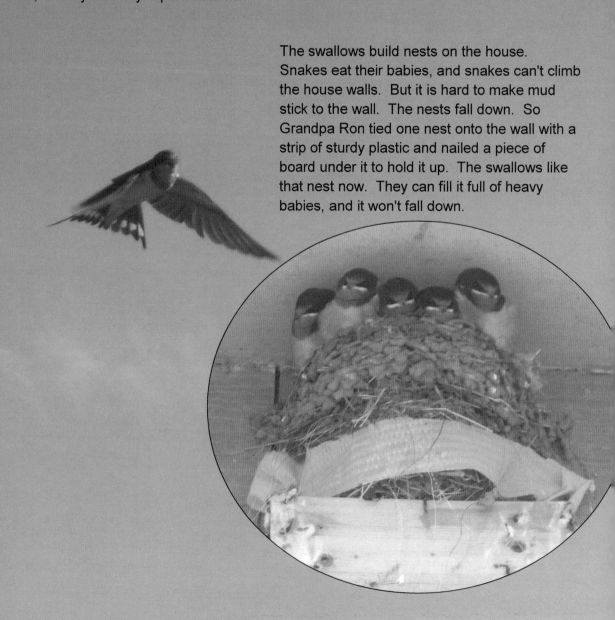

Once we had one cold day. The mosquitoes all hid. The new baby swallows were dying. They could not go all day without food. Grandma Rose soaked cat chow and gave it to them. Cat chow has a lot of protein like mosquitoes do. The baby swallows got better, and the next day there were more mosquitoes.

The swallows like the barn, too. It has water for our animals. It has lots of mosquitoes, because they like to bite milk cows and horses.

Sometimes we have really hot days. The baby swallows get too hot. They flop over the sides of their nests and pant. Grandma Rose takes a spray bottle with water and sprays them. At first they are afraid, but they learn Grandma Rose is their friend.

We have to take good care of our swallows. In the fall they leave us and fly south. Not everyone in the south has been careful. Our swallows can't always find a safe, clean place to spend the winter. A lot die. We want there to always be swallows. So we have to take good care of them when they are with us.

Bullsnakes eat swallows. We don't like that, but we do like our bullsnakes. Bullsnakes are big. They are pretty and a little spooky.

Bullsnakes eat mice. Some mice have nasty diseases that can make people really sick. And bullsnakes make rattlesnakes stay out of the yard. Rattlesnakes in the yard are dangerous.

Bullsnakes hatch from big, soft eggs. Grandma Rose found a bullsnake that died right after it hatched. We don't know what happened to it, but it looked really neat.

This year a badger found a bullsnake nest. It dug the eggs up. We tried to rebury them and save them, but it didn't work. Sixty-six baby bullsnakes died in their eggs. They never got a chance to be alive at all. We were sorry. But badgers are neat, too.

This winter we saw a little porcupine. He wasn't afraid of us, because he showed us his belly. Their bellies are soft and don't have quills. If they are afraid, they curl up to protect their bellies. And he talked to us. He sounded a little bit like a cat.

Beaver are fun to watch, too. They build big dams and lodges and long, smooth canals. This is the front door to a big beaver lodge. The beaver weren't using it this year, so we went to look at it.

We saw baby beaver in the spring. In winter, we saw a porcupine go into a beaver lodge. I don't know what the beaver thought about that.

The beaver chop down a lot of the cottonwood trees. We don't want there to be no trees left, so Grandpa Ron puts wire around some of the trees. Then the beaver will leave them alone. Sometimes.

To have a garden, we have to carry water.
Sometimes Linden and I help. It is a lot of
work. Water is rare on the prairie, so it's
important to respect it. It's important to
respect food, too, because it takes water to
make food, and something has to die so
you can eat. When I was two, I asked
Mommy why we killed the cows and the
carrots and ate them. We are like the owls
that kill the mice and eat them. We can't
make what we eat healthier by eating it the
way the grazers can. But we can help the
grazers do their job better. I like being part
of something important.

There is always a lot of work to do on the ranch, but I don't work all the time. I like to read best of all.

I tried to learn to spin wool into yarn, but it's hard.

I also like to make things. I draw and paint. I knitted a dress for my doll.

For kindergarten, I wove snowshoes from rawhide. Grandpa Ron made the rawhide. He braids beautiful hackamores for the horses from rawhide. He made the hackamore that Trisca and I use. He let me use some of his extra rawhide for the snowshoes. They worked OK, but we fell down a lot and sometimes they fell off.

I also wove a cradle board for my dolls from willows. I used a piece of deerskin that Mommy tanned when she was a little girl.

I like to play the piano and sing.

Sometimes Linden and I help Mommy or Daddy or Grandma Rose cook.

Daddy built a swing set for
Linden and me. It is lots of fun.

We have to go to town to get clothes and store food and our mail. Sometimes we go to town for fun things. We go to the Summer Theater for one play every year. Mommy and I tried to go to Shakespeare in the Parks once, but they had a tornado warning instead. It was interesting, but kind of scary. I would rather have had the play.

On the Fourth of July, there is a parade that Linden and I can be in with Mommy. There are games and a big picnic and pie. Linden used to be allergic to pie, so he really likes the Fourth of July now.

94 Years
Toughing   Timber
It Out on   Creek

There is a parade on Labor Day, too. They have a picnic and games and JohnDMagician has a magic show. This year, he let Linden and me help him.

There was even a Ferris wheel.

In the fall, there is a picnic and dance at Juneberg Bridge. Grandpa Ron had two little girls, so he always had to dance all the time. He thought that when Mommy and my aunt got married, they could dance with their husbands. But Daddy plays in the band. So Mommy still has to dance with Grandpa Ron or with us.

This is the year I was five. Daddy is on the far end of the stage in the black sweater. Linden and I are dancing with Kodi. Grandma and Grandpa are dancing beside us. They are really good dancers. This year Daddy sang, too. He sang a silly song and made all the people laugh.

The County Fair is lots of fun. We play games with the other kids. We get to see all the animals and pretty things people bring to the Fair. We get to ride at the carnival. I put the dress that I knitted for Molly Dolly in the Fair. It won a rosette for Best First Project.

I had kindergarten at home with Mommy. Now that I am a big girl, I have home school and real school both. Four of us go to real school, Lindy and I and A.J. and her little brother, Thatcher. There are not any other buildings by our school. Our school is almost as old as our ranch. A.J.'s mommy and grandma and great grandma went to school there. So did Grandma Rose.

It was hard for Grandma Rose to go to school. The kids had to drive to school by themselves. The pick-up didn't have a heater. If they got stuck, they had to shovel out without help.

The first time we got stuck, I was scared, because I remembered Grandma Rose's stories, but it wasn't too bad. The car was nice and warm. Mommy did all the shoveling for us. She said that if Linden and I kept arguing, we would have to get out and help her, but we decided not to argue any more.

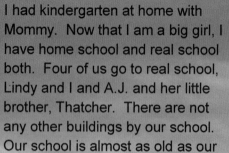

The day the snow was really deep and we got really, really stuck, I did help, though. Linden and I stomped a path for the car while Mommy shoveled. A.J.'s grandma came looking for us. Our neighbor Eva heard we hadn't come to school when she went for her mail, so she came looking, too. She is A.J.'s great great aunt... I think. Everybody had to shovel a lot, but we all got out of the drift in the end. Mommy has only had to shovel six times. I don't think she's as good a driver as Daddy, but I don't want her to feel bad, because I know she tries hard.

This is our class.

Linden and I helped to get the school room ready this fall.

All of us worked to get our school clean for our Christmas program.

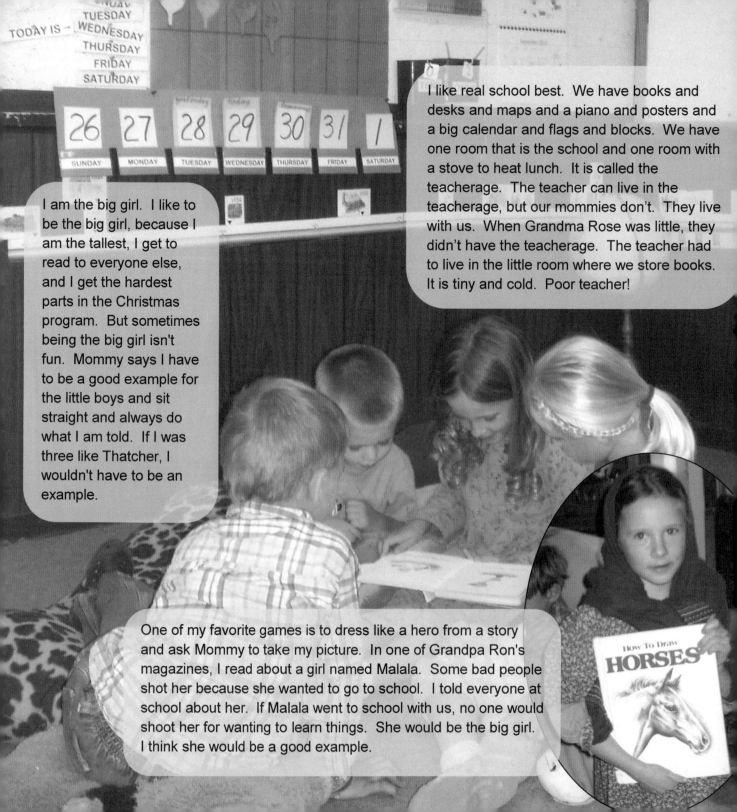

TODAY IS –
TUESDAY
WEDNESDAY
THURSDAY
FRIDAY
SATURDAY

| 26 | 27 | 28 | 29 | 30 | 31 | 1 |
| SUNDAY | MONDAY | TUESDAY | WEDNESDAY | THURSDAY | FRIDAY | SATURDAY |

I like real school best. We have books and desks and maps and a piano and posters and a big calendar and flags and blocks. We have one room that is the school and one room with a stove to heat lunch. It is called the teacherage. The teacher can live in the teacherage, but our mommies don't. They live with us. When Grandma Rose was little, they didn't have the teacherage. The teacher had to live in the little room where we store books. It is tiny and cold. Poor teacher!

I am the big girl. I like to be the big girl, because I am the tallest, I get to read to everyone else, and I get the hardest parts in the Christmas program. But sometimes being the big girl isn't fun. Mommy says I have to be a good example for the little boys and sit straight and always do what I am told. If I was three like Thatcher, I wouldn't have to be an example.

One of my favorite games is to dress like a hero from a story and ask Mommy to take my picture. In one of Grandpa Ron's magazines, I read about a girl named Malala. Some bad people shot her because she wanted to go to school. I told everyone at school about her. If Malala went to school with us, no one would shoot her for wanting to learn things. She would be the big girl. I think she would be a good example.

HOW TO DRAW
HORSES

When I'm big, I want to go to college like Mommy and Daddy and Grandpa and Grandma. I like to learn about how dead plants and animals turn into new soil, so maybe I will study that. I want to visit the Czech Republic so I can practice speaking Czech. Maybe I will be an actress and learn to talk like Shakespeare.

But right now I love living on the ranch. I love seeing the plants and birds and animals. I love having important jobs.